DATE DUE

JA 21 77			
MY 13 77			
JE 10 77			
JA 20 '78			
JA 27 '78			
MR 3 78			

D1095702

JUVENILE
QL568
A6K67

1978

RIVERSIDE C C LIBRARY

THE
BUSY HONEYBEE

by Bernice Kohn
Illustrated by Mel Furukawa

FOUR WINDS PRESS   NEW YORK

PUBLISHED BY FOUR WINDS PRESS

A DIVISION OF SCHOLASTIC MAGAZINES, INC., NEW YORK, N.Y.

TEXT COPYRIGHT © 1972 BY BERNICE KOHN

ILLUSTRATIONS COPYRIGHT © 1972 BY MEL FURUKAWA
ALL RIGHTS RESERVED.
PRINTED IN THE UNITED STATES OF AMERICA

LIBRARY OF CONGRESS CATALOGUE CARD NUMBER: 72-77806

There are more than 50,000 honeybees in this swarm. They are waiting on the tree while their scouts look for a new nesting place.

The bees are gathered around their queen. She is the most important bee in the colony. The others are called workers and drones.

Honeybees, unlike some other kinds of bees, always live in colonies. They are excellent honey producers and are the bees that are kept by beekeepers.

Although not all bees are honeybees, all bees are insects. They have three body parts: a head, a thorax, and an abdomen. They also have six legs, four wings and hairy bodies.

There are two feelers, or antennae, on the front of a bee's head. The bee uses them to touch things and for smelling, too, since it has no nose.

And a bee's head has two very large eyes. They are called compound eyes because they are like thousands of tiny eyes put together. Between the two large eyes there are three small ones.

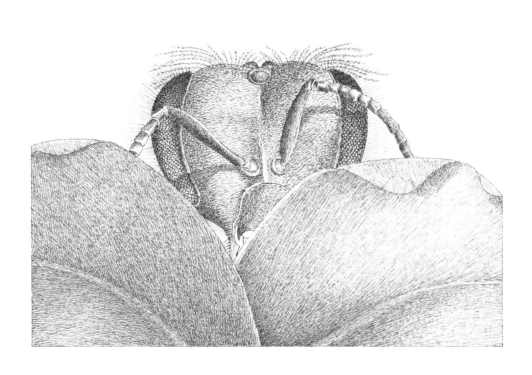

In some ways, different kinds of honeybees are different from each other. This is a worker bee. One of her many jobs is to gather nectar and pollen. She has a long tongue that works like a soda straw. She can push it into a flower and suck up the nectar. She gathers pollen at the same time because it sticks to the hairs on her body. Before she flies away, she packs the pollen into the pollen baskets on her rear legs.

Another of the worker's jobs is to make wax. Wax comes from glands called wax plates on the underside of the bee's abdomen.

At the end of her tail she has a stinger to attack her enemies, such as the praying mantis on the opposite page.

This bee is a drone. He is larger than a worker. His eyes are larger, too, and meet at the top of his head. He has no pollen baskets and no wax plates. His tongue is not long enough to sip nectar. He doesn't even have a stinger. He is fed by the workers and has no work to do. His only job is to mate with the queen.

When the summer is over and honey is scarce, the workers chase the drones from the nest and they die.

The queen is the largest honeybee. Although she starts life as a plain worker egg, she quickly gets special care. The egg has extra space around it. As soon as it hatches into a grub, or larva, it is fed royal jelly. This is special "queen food" that the workers make in their mouths.

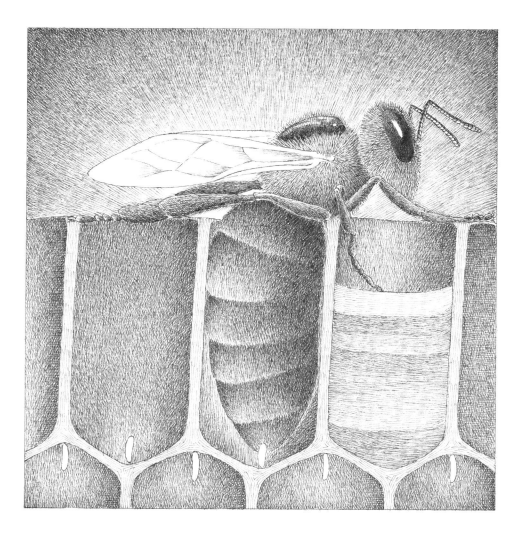

In about a week the queen larva spins a silky cocoon. Now she is called a pupa. In another week she has grown into a queen bee and comes out of her cell.

The first thing she does is look for other queen cells. When she finds one, she stings the growing queen to death.

When she is the only queen left alive, she takes to the air.

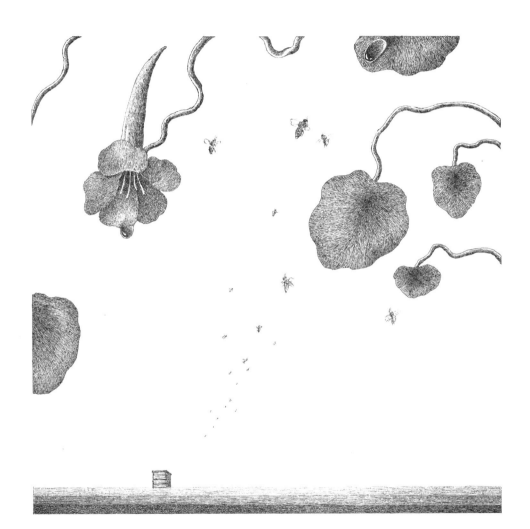

This is the queen's mating flight. She picks one of the many drones who follow her into the air and mates with him. Then she comes back to the hive to lay her eggs. She lays thousands and thousands of eggs. No other bee in the hive will ever produce eggs to keep the hive alive.

A hive is a man-made nest for bees. It is usually a wooden box with two or more stories. Bees that don't find hives nest in caves and hollow trees.

The expression "busy as a bee hive" is a good one. A bee hive is a very busy place. All the work is done by worker bees. The first thing they do in a new hive is build a comb.

They hang themselves up like a curtain and scrape wax from their wax plates. Then they chew it until it is soft and use it to build a comb made of six-sided cells. Some of the cells are used to store honey. Some are used as nurseries for eggs or young bees.

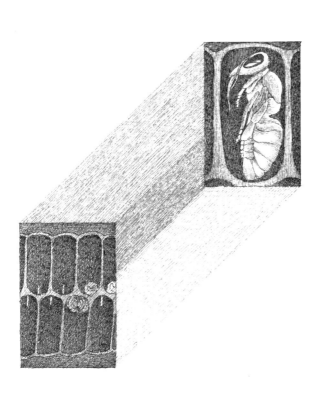

The queen lays one egg in each cell. After a few days the eggs hatch into tiny, white larvae. For two days the workers feed them all royal jelly. After that only queen larvae get queen food. Workers and drones are fed a mixture of honey and pollen called bee bread.

In about a week, each larva grows into a pupa. It spins a cocoon and, snug inside, grows into a bee. This takes about two weeks. And in two weeks more, the worker bees are ready to start their jobs. They clean dust and scraps from cells and build a new comb. They guard the hive from enemies such as bears, mice and other honey-loving animals. When the hive gets too hot, the workers cool it by fanning it with their wings. The workers are nursemaids to the larvae and to the queen.

One of the workers' most important jobs is gathering nectar and pollen from flowers. As soon as workers return to the hive they brush the pollen from their pollen baskets. It is packed into cells and stored until it is needed.

But the nectar is not ready for use. The workers bring it to the hive in their honey stomachs. These are not real stomachs where digestion takes place, but storage bins. Each worker empties her nectar, which is a thin liquid, into comb cells. The cells are left open to the air. After a while, the nectar changes into thick honey and then the workers seal the cells with wax.

Since pollen and nectar are the bees' food, the insects must always have a good supply of flowers. Some workers are flower scouts. When they find new ones they return to the nest to let the other bees know. They communicate this with a dance.

If the food is near the nest, the scout does a round dance. She goes around and around in small circles, first one way, then the other. All the bees grow very excited. When the scout stops her dance and flies back to the flowers, the other workers follow.

If the flowers are far from the nest, the dance is not such a simple one. It is called a wagging dance. This dance must tell the other bees which way to go and how far to fly.

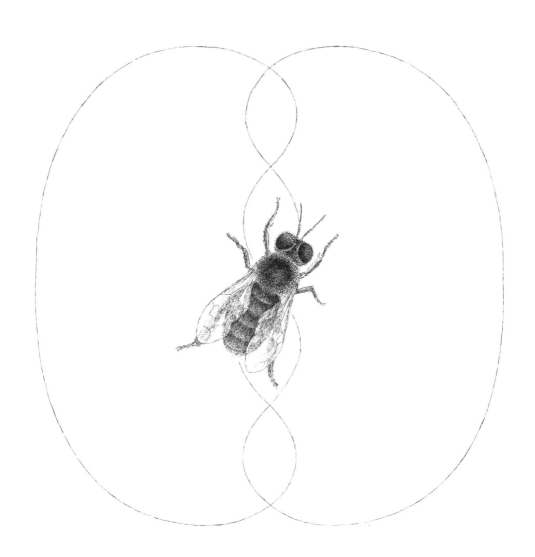

The wagging dance is in two parts. First, the bee dashes straight ahead, wagging her abdomen as she goes. The direction she takes shows which way to go. It may be toward the sun, away from the sun, or to the right or left of it.

In the second part of the dance, the bee makes two circles, first in one direction, then in the other. The length of the line between the two circles tells the other bees how far they have to fly.

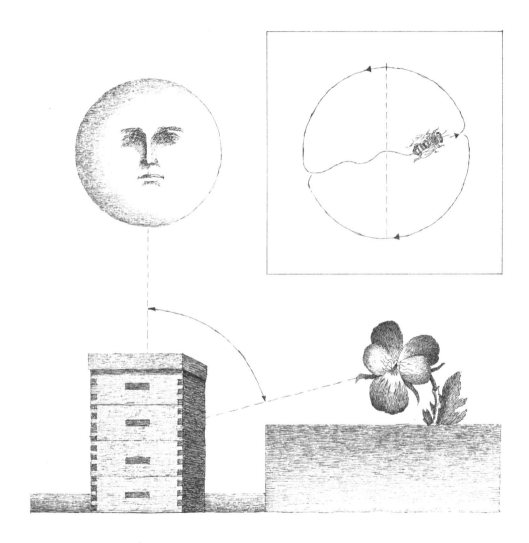

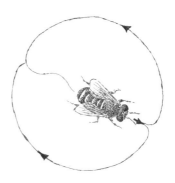

Bees dance when they find a new home, too. The swarm pictured at the beginning of this book was waiting for a scout to come back and dance to tell them where to find a new hive.

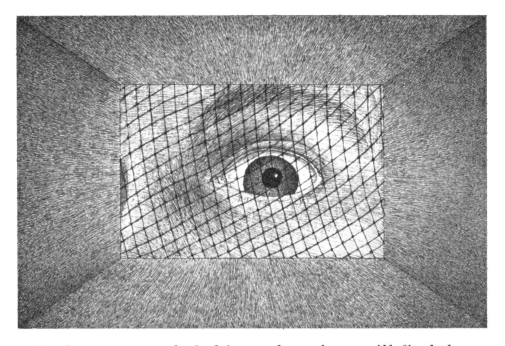

Beekeepers put their hives where bees will find them easily. When the bees have stored all the honey they need for themselves, the beekeeper takes the "leftovers." He puts the honey into jars and sends it to stores.

Beekeeping is not a new art. Bee farms, or *apiaries,* were known in ancient times. It became possible to handle bees when someone discovered that the insects grew very quiet when the hive was filled with smoke.

Beekeepers still use smoke when they collect honey. Although the men usually cover their skin, they are not often stung. They even handle swarming bees to coax them into a new hive. When a few bees enter the hive the rest of the swarm follows.

The earliest man-made hives were hollow logs. Later, they were made of straw, woven rush, pottery or wood. All of these are still used in some parts of the world. However, the most popular kind of hive is a wooden one with movable frames, each holding one comb. The combs are hung in the hive with space for the bees to move under and around them. When the beekeeper collects honey, he can lift out a single comb without disturbing the rest of the hive. There are probably more than five million hives in North America today. Five million hives, all filled with honey!

Some of it, honey for bees—and some of it, honey for people.

H*O*N*E*Y

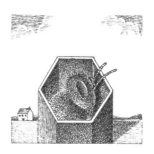